Contents

Who was A. A. Milne? 4

Where did he grow up? 6

What did he do before he
    was a writer? 8

How did he start writing books? 10

What books did he write? 12

What did he write about? 14

Who drew the pictures in
    A. A. Milne's books? 16

What else did A. A. Milne do? 18

Why is he famous today? 20

Timeline of A. A. Milne's life and work . . . 22

Glossary 23

Find out more 24

Index 24

Some words are shown in bold, **like this**. You can find them in the glossary on page 23.

Who was A. A. Milne?

A. A. Milne was a writer.

He wrote stories and **poems** for children.

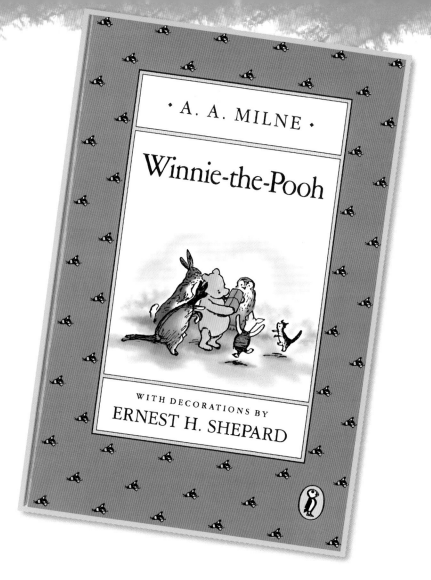

His full name was Alan Alexander Milne.

His most famous book is called
Winnie-the-Pooh.

Where did he grow up?

A. A. Milne was born in 1882.

He lived in London, England.

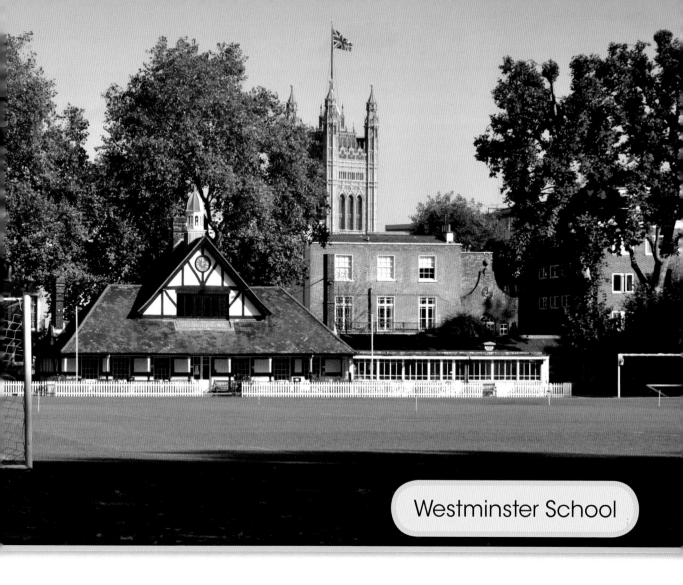

Westminster School

A. A. Milne grew up in the school where his father was a teacher.

Then he went to a famous school in London.

What did he do before he was a writer?

World War 1 started in 1914.

A. A. Milne joined the army and went to fight in France.

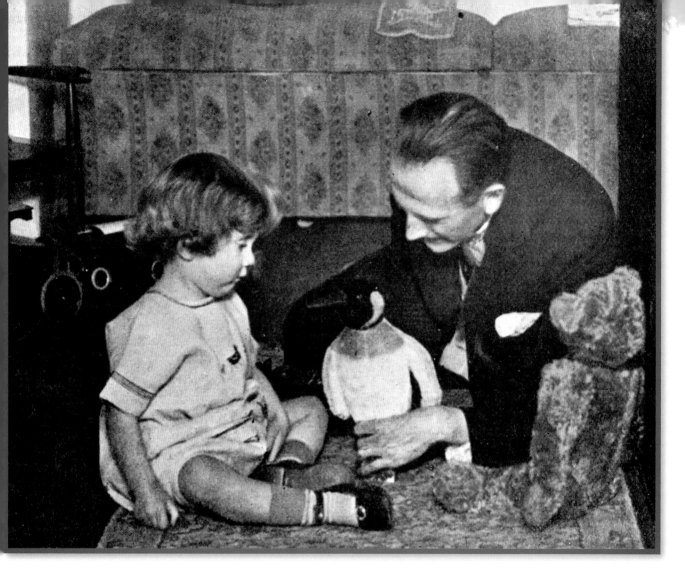

After the war, A. A. Milne returned home to write **plays**.

Then he had a son called Christopher Robin.

How did he start writing books?

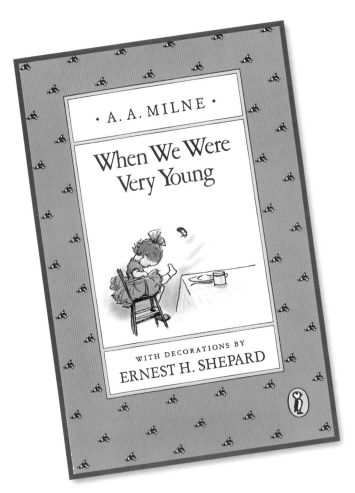

A. A. Milne wrote poetry for children that was **published** in magazines.

His **poems** were put together in a book called *When We Were Very Young*.

Then he wrote a book of stories called *Winnie-the-Pooh*.

Winnie-the-Pooh was Christopher Robin's toy bear.

What books did he write?

A. A. Milne wrote two other books for children.

The House at Pooh Corner was also about Winnie-the-Pooh and his friends.

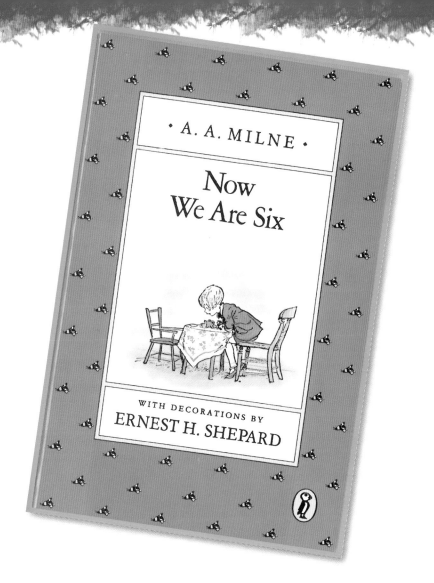

Now We Are Six was another **collection** of **poems**.

A. A. Milne also wrote some **plays** for adults.

What did he write about?

A. A. Milne's poetry was usually funny.

His **poems** were often about young children exploring the world.

A. A. Milne's stories were about his son Christopher Robin.

Christopher Robin's toy animals were also in these funny stories.

Who drew the pictures in A. A. Milne's books?

A. A. Milne did not draw the pictures in his books.

Ernest H. Shepard was an artist who drew the pictures.

Some of Ernest's pictures are black and white **line drawings**.

Other pictures are painted in colour.

What else did A. A. Milne do?

A. A. Milne also wrote films and **plays**.

He used the book *The Wind in the Willows* to write a play called *Toad of Toad Hall*.

A. A. Milne was not well when he got older.

He liked living in the country and reading books.

Why is he famous today?

People still buy A. A. Milne's books today.

Many children see his characters in cartoon films and on television.

Disney intellectual property used with permission from Disney Enterprises, Inc. Based on the "Winnie the Pooh" works, by A.A. Milne and E.H. Shepard.

You can see toys of these characters in the shops.

People still write books and magazines about them, too.

Timeline of A. A. Milne's life and work

1882	A. A. Milne was born in London.
1916	A. A. Milne went to France to fight in **World War 1**.
1920	Christopher Robin was born.
1924	*When We Were Very Young* was **published**.
1926	*Winnie-the-Pooh* was published.
1927	*Now We Are Six* was published.
1928	*The House at Pooh Corner* was published.
1956	A. A. Milne died.

Glossary

collection group of things put together

line drawing picture made of dark lines, done with a pen or pencil

play story that is acted out

poem piece of writing that puts ideas or feelings into words. Some poems rhyme.

published made into a book or put in a magazine and printed

World War 1 a big war that lasted for more than four years

Find out more

Books

Books by A. A. Milne and E.H. Shepard: *When We Were Very Young, Winnie-the-Pooh, Now We Are Six,* and *The House at Pooh Corner.*

Websites

www.poohcorner.com
Visit this website to find out more about A. A. Milne and Christopher Robin.

Index

book 5, 10, 11, 12–13, 16, 18, 19, 20, 21

Christopher Robin 9, 11, 15

collection 13, 23

Ernest H. Shepard 16–17

picture 16, 17, 23

play 9, 13, 18, 23

poem 4, 10, 13, 14, 23

World War 1 8, 9, 22, 23